This book is to be returned on or befo:

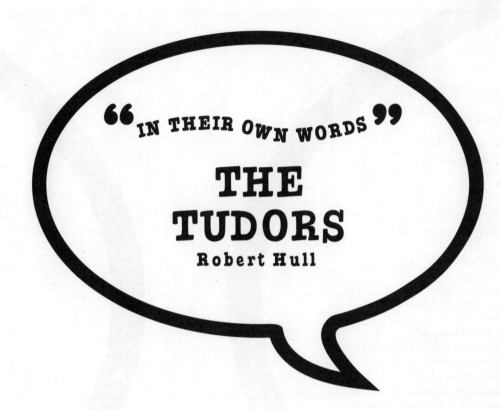

" IN THEIR OWN WORDS "

THE TUDORS

Robert Hull

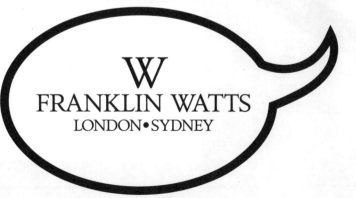

W
FRANKLIN WATTS
LONDON • SYDNEY

First published in 2001 by
Franklin Watts
96 Leonard Street
EC2A 4XD

Franklin Watts Australia
56 O'Riordan Street
Alexandria
NSW 2015

Series editor: Rachel Cooke
Editor: Sarah Ridley
Designer: Jason Anscomb
Consultant: Mrs Barbara Searle
Illustrations: Mike White
Cover images: Erich Lessing/
Kunsthistorisches Museum, Vienna/AKG
London: front & back covers bl & br.
Whilst every attempt has been made to clear
copyright should there be an inadvertent
omission please apply in the first instance to
the publisher regarding rectification.

A CIP catalogue record for this book
is available from the British Library.

ISBN 0 7496 4070 7

Dewey Classification 942.05

Printed in Malaysia

"IN THEIR OWN WORDS"

Introduction

The Tudor kings and queens ruled from 1485, when Henry Tudor came to the throne at the end of the Wars of the Roses, until 1603, when Elizabeth I died. James Stuart (James I of England and VI of Scotland) then united Wales and England with Scotland.

The Tudor period was a time of great change. Education expanded, with many schools and colleges being built, and lots of books published. There were new industries and a building boom, especially under Henry VIII. Ambitious journeys of exploration, like Francis Drake's voyage round the world, led to increased trade with many parts of the world, and the setting up of colonies.

The horizons of Tudor people's thinking broadened. Far-away countries and continents became part of the Tudor mental picture. Merchants travelled not just to trade but to learn industrial secrets. With new things round them, and so much being printed in English, Tudor people became more curious. Many new science books were published.

A list of some Tudor 'firsts' suggests how fast all this change took place: the first national Atlas in the world, the first maps of Britain, the first English river to be dug out for the use of shipping, the first sonnet in English, the first church service in English and the first permanent playhouse.

Perhaps the most important change was in religion. The Church of Henry VII's time was Roman Catholic[1], with bishops appointed by the Pope in Rome. People began to question the Pope's authority and suggest a new approach to religion. In a process known as the Reformation[2], various European Churches broke away from Rome, including England. In 1534, because of his quarrel with the Pope over a divorce from Catherine of Aragon, Henry VIII became head of the English Church and, by 1603, the Protestant[3] Church of England was well established.

These changes meant that religion and politics became closely linked, and people who did not agree with the religious changes were regarded by the government as

1. **Roman Catholic:** Christian Church with the Pope in Rome as its leader.
2. **the Reformation:** the 'reforming' of Christian belief that took place in the 16th century.
3. **Protestant:** the name given to those Christian Churches that separated from the Roman Catholic Church in the 16th century and followed the beliefs of the Reformation.

4

traitors. Henry VIII had some 300 people executed because they opposed his new power over the Church. Henry's daughter Mary Tudor tried to restore the Catholic faith in England. She had 300 people burnt for their Protestant beliefs.

Tudor England was an exciting and sometimes dangerous place. There were several rebellions and plots against the Crown, some connected with the religious changes and some to do with high taxes, new farming practices and unpopular rulers. By the end of the period, despite everything, the country was far more secure and prosperous than at the beginning.

The big ships of the Tudor navy protected its prosperity, at one point repelling a great Spanish Armada[4]. Small ships voyaged thousands of miles, raiding, exploring, even sailing to Newfoundland for fish.

However, not everyone enjoyed Tudor prosperity. When Thomas More was earning £400 a year, a landless country labourer's wage was pegged at 18s 6d (91p)[5] a year. Then, in the middle of the century, with many wages fixed, the price of food and other things went up. When land was enclosed for sheep-farming, many country labourers lost their homes and their work. Beggars became common, even a threat.

Passing scattered villages, time-travellers would meet these wandering vagabonds, and see the great flocks of sheep that displaced many of them. They would find the countryside very different from ours, more isolated and wild, but with more wild flowers, animals and birds, untouched woods and wasteland.

4. **Armada**: a great fleet of warships.
5. **18s 6d**: 18 shillings and 16 pence. There were 20 shillings to the pound and 12 pence in each shilling. In today's money, a shilling equals 5p, but in real terms it was worth a great deal more, as these earnings suggest.

Written Records from Tudor England

William Caxton set up his printing press in London in 1474, eleven years before the first Tudor king. Books poured from the press through Tudor times: travel books, farming manuals, books of manners, political books and religious books complaining about the people's wicked ways. Many thousands of titles had appeared in English by 1601, including books translated from other languages.

But even when Elizabeth I came to the throne, only about 20% of men and 5% of women could sign their names, let alone read. People communicated their ideas by talking and listening, which is why plays were so popular.

During the medieval period, French and Latin had been widely used for written records. Now the English language finally took over – in law-courts, churches, books, even in grammar schools[1] some of the time. Monarchs still talked in Latin with visitors from abroad and scholars often wrote their books in Latin, though even amongst them English became more popular. The English language expanded rapidly.

In this exciting time of experimentation and creativity, Tudor kings and queens wrote a great deal, both about political matters and more personal details, not only letters, but also in poems and songs.

State officials recorded huge amounts of material on a wide range of issues affecting the government. For example, there were royal commissions investigating such matters as whether the iron industry in Sussex should be closed down for damage to the environment. Law-courts wrote down accounts of trials and the judgements given there. We can even read what rebels wrote down in petitions presented to the king and what teachers wrote for pupils to translate into Latin.

People visiting foreign countries often write down impressions of what they see. Fascinating letters and journals were written in Tudor England by lone travellers, by refugees who settled and worked in England, and by numerous officials on political business from Italy, Spain or elsewhere.

And of course there was a poetry and play explosion. Shakespeare and a hundred others recorded their age for us in language we remember. We can often understand Shakespeare and other writers without translating them into modern English. The quotes in this book are often in the original Tudor English with just the spelling modernized, but sometimes we have sometimes modernized the language to make the quotations clearer.

1. **grammar school:** so called because grammar was the main subject taught.

Biographies of the Main Contributors

Roger Ascham (1515-1568) was a private tutor to Princess Elizabeth, and a lecturer at Cambridge University. He wrote *The Schoolmaster – a plain and perfect way of teaching children to understand, write and speak in the Latin tongue*, which was published in 1570.

John Foxe (1517-1587) was a writer and a churchman in Salisbury. His book *Actes and Monuments* (which came to be called *Foxe's Martyrs*) became extremely popular as soon as it appeared in 1563. It especially celebrates Protestants[2] martyred under Mary I.

Richard Hakluyt (1552-1616) wrote books about voyages of exploration, including *Principal Navigations, Voyages and Discoveries*, published in 1589 that became well-known. He was also closely connected with the Muscovy Company[3].

William Harrison (1534-1593) was a church rector. His *Description of England* published in 1577 and revised in 1587, is one of the most valuable pictures of England written at the time.

Sir Thomas More (1478-1535) was a politician, lawyer and writer. He became Lord Chancellor in 1529 but fell out of favour with Henry VIII because he disapproved publicly of Henry's divorce and his weakening of the Pope's power in England. He was imprisoned in the Tower of London, put on trial and executed. His famous book *Utopia* meaning 'no-place' came out in 1516.

Thomas Platter (1574-1628) was a Swiss traveller who came to England in 1599 and kept a detailed journal of his visit. As a visitor to a strange land, his observations on London, travel and the country provide fascinating reading.

Sir Walter Raleigh (1522-1618) was a poet, politician, explorer and soldier. He found favour at the court of Elizabeth I.

Hugh Rhodes (active c. 1550) wrote his *Boke of Nurture, or the School of Good Manners* for the children of the King's chapel.

Philip Stubbes (active 1583-1591) was a Puritan[4] pamphleteer and writer. His book *Anatomy of Abuses* (1583) is an attack on all kinds of things Puritans disliked, such as fashion, dancing, games and plays, but also on cruel sports.

2. Protestant: see page 4.

3. Muscovy Company: trading company concerned with trade with Russia.

4. Puritan: a Protestant believer who wanted to rid the Church and everyday life of rituals and ceremonies felt to be Catholic.

Kings and Queens

Tudor kings and queens had more power than kings and queens do now. It was they personally who governed the country, making decisions that today would be made by ministers or by Parliament. Tudor people expected their kings and queens to rule. They expected the monarch to lead, to decide whether to go to war and what laws to change. If people objected, they also knew that opposition to the will of the monarch would be treason, punishable by death.

Although Tudor kings and queens were powerful, they could not rule without Parliament and during the 16th century Parliament became more and more important. The changes in the Church were made through Acts of Parliament and, because of the war against Spain, Elizabeth I had to regularly ask Parliament for money. The role Parliament played laid the foundations for what it does today. Despite this, Tudor kings and queens held sway over Parliament, and could use force if necessary. No-one in Parliament had legal immunity from royal anger. Opposing the monarch's wishes might mean losing one's head.

Through their power and personalities, monarchs shaped the country in different ways. This led to ups and downs, but it also created the excitement and energy of the Tudor age.

Henry VII (reigned 1485-1509)

Being accepted as the rightful ruler was one problem that Tudor monarchs faced. Henry VII had to unmask impersonators claiming to be the heir of Edward IV, and to prevent England's wealth from draining away in war. Henry impressed Polydore Vergil, an Italian who was at Henry's court from 1502. He wrote this in his *English History*.

In government he was shrewd and far-seeing, so that none dared to get the better of him by deceit or sharp practice. Above all else he cherished justice; and he punished with the utmost rigour robberies, murders, and every other kind of crime.

Polydore Vergil, 1534

1. **butts**: place where targets were placed for archery practice.
2. **13s 4d**: see page 5.
3. **the fool**: comedian-style entertainer.
4. **drone**: a wind instrument that played a continuous note, like a bagpipe.
5. **vamplat**: circular plate fixed on a spear or lance to protect the hand.
6. **Abbot of Misrule**: entertainer who led wild celebrations on certain feast days.
7. **cossacks**: Russian dancers.
8. **Shrovetide**: religious festival held on Shrove Tuesday (Pancake Day).
9. **Catholic**: see Roman Catholic, page 4.

Henry VII looked after the country's money carefully; England was well-off financially after his reign. Henry himself signed this record of payments for court entertainments, made by John Heron, King's Treasurer.

1492
June 4th Item to Sir Edward Borough which the king lost at butts[1] with his crossbow 13s 4d[2]
June 10th Item to a Spaniard that played the fool[3] 40s
June 11th Item to one that played upon the drone[4] 6s 8d
June 17th Item to Master Guyfford for spears, spearheads and vamplats[5] bought for the jousts £9 6s
June 30th to the king which he lost at cards 40s
August 1st Item to the children for singing in the garden 3s 4d
October 24th Item to Ringeley, Abbot of Misrule[6] 100s
1493
January 6th Item to Newark for making of a song 20s
March 2nd Item to Master Bray for rewards to them that brought cossacks[7] at Shrovetide[8] at Westminster 20s
March 22nd Item to the fool, the Duke of Lancaster 10s
May 16th Item to Pudesey Piper on the bagpipe 6s 8d
1494
January 2nd Item for playing of the morris dance 40s
January 6th Item for clothing mad Dick the fool 35s 7d
May 29th Item to one that tumbled before the king 20s
June 13th Item to a Spaniard the tennis player £4

Court Expenses, 1492-94

Henry VIII (reigned 1509-1547)

Henry VIII was obsessed with the need for a male heir; Anne Boleyn might give him one, but to marry her he had to get a divorce from Catherine of Aragon, his wife. The Pope would not grant this, so Henry became the head of the Church in England, though services initially remained Catholic[9]. That way he could decree who was to remain married or be divorced.

Henry VIII, aged 24, made a great impression on the diplomat, Pasqualigo, who described him in a report to Venice.

We at length reached the king, who was under a canopy of cloth of gold, embroidered in Florence, the most costly thing I have ever seen. He was leaning against his gilt throne, on which there was a large gold brocade cushion, where the long gold sword of state lay. He wore a cap of crimson velvet, in the French fashion, and the brim was looped up all round with laces, which had gold enamel tags... Very close round his neck he had a gold collar, from which there hung a round cut diamond, the size of the largest walnut I ever saw, and from this was suspended a most beautiful very large round pearl.

Lorenzo Pasqualigo, 1515

State papers show how the young king spent his time – from wrestling, to writing music.

... exercising himself daily in shooting, singing, dancing, wrestling, casting at the bar, playing recorders, flutes, virginals[1] and setting of songs.

State Papers, 1509-47

1. **virginals:** keyboard instrument.

Henry's letters to Anne Boleyn, who became his second wife, show how much he was in love with her at the time. He sent her a picture of himself.

Seeing that I cannot be in your presence, I send you now the thing most nearly there to appertaining that it is possible to send, which is my picture in a bracelet...

He was in 'distress', not knowing from her letters how she felt about him.

Debating with myself the contents of your letters, I have put myself in great distress, not knowing how to interpret them, whether to my disadvantage, as in some places is shown, or to advantage, as in others I understand them; praying you with all my heart that you will expressly certify me of your whole mind concerning the love between us two.

Henry VIII, 1527-1528

Edward VI (reigned 1547-1553)

On the death of his father, Henry VIII, Edward VI became king at the age of nine. As he was so young, regents helped him rule throughout his life including his uncle, the Duke of Somerset, who acted as Regent until 1549. Edward died young in 1553 at the age of 15. The following quotes are entries from the diary he kept. This brief, chilly entry recorded the execution of the Duke of Somerset.

The Duke of Somerset had his head cut off upon Tower Hill between 8 and 9 o'clock in the morning.

Edward realised his youth had been taken advantage of.

The Lord Paget, Chancellor of the Duchy of Lancaster, confessed how he, without commission to do so, sold off some of my land and some great timber woods; how he took huge rents from my lands for his own private profit and advantage, failing to hand them over for my use and enjoyment.

Edward VI, 1552

Edward VI was said to have been a brilliant boy. An Italian doctor, Giralamo Cardano, who visited Edward when he knew he was dying, found him 'an extraordinary person'.

He could speak many languages when he was still a child. As well as English, his first language, he spoke Latin and French. And I gather that he knew Greek, Italian and Spanish… He was a marvellous young man. When I saw him he was fifteen, and he spoke Latin as well and as confidently as I did… When the stately seriousness of the King was called for, his demeanour was that of a mature grown man. And yet he was always easy-going and polite, as befitted his youth. He played on the lute[2], and he also intervened in matters of state, as his father had done; though whereas the father, in attempting to be too good, seems to have been bad, the son could not be suspected of that, for his mind was developed by the study of philosophy.

Giralamo Cardano, 1553

2. **lute**: stringed instrument popular at the time.

11

Mary I (reigned 1553-1558)

The fervent Queen Mary was determined to make the country Catholic[1] again on the death of her Protestant[2] brother. She died before she could finish her project, and had no children. The reputation and stature of the monarchy, as well as its financial strength, suffered from the short reigns of Edward VI and Mary I.

The Italian ambassador, Giacomo Soranzo, painted in a letter this word-picture of Mary before she came to the throne, stressing the strength of her Catholic belief.

She is so committed to the Catholic religion that although the King, her brother, prohibited her from having mass celebrated according to the Roman Catholic ritual, she nevertheless had it performed in secret. She never acknowledged in any way the truth of any other form of religion. Her belief in the religion she had been born into was so strong that if need be she would have exhibited it at the stake. Her Majesty takes great pleasure in playing the lute[3] and the spinet[4], and she plays both instruments very well... But more than anything she seems to enjoy dressing elegantly and magnificently.

Giacomo Soranzo, 1554

1. **Catholic:** see page 4.
2. **Protestant:** see page 4.
3. **lute:** see page 11.
4. **spinet:** keyboard instrument.

Towards the end of her reign there was a rumour that Mary had given birth; she died later after an illness which she thought was a pregnancy. The Protestant writer, John Foxe, suspected a plot to produce a Catholic heir.

It was believed to be nearly the time when this young master would be born into the world, and midwives and nurses with the cradle and rockers and everyone else were prepared and in readiness. Then suddenly, for what reason or on what provocation is uncertain, a silly rumour blew into London that the Queen had been happily delivered of a child... Various preachers, particularly one, the parson of St Anne in Aldergate, after a procession and the singing of a Te Deum[5],

5. **Te Deum:** an anthem to God.

took it upon himself to describe the child's features and appearance, say how handsome, how beautiful, how splendid a prince he was. In the end it all turned out to be the opposite of the truth. The happiness and hopeful expectations of people were turned upside down. They were told that the queen had not only not had a child, but she had no hope of having one.

John Foxe, 1563

Elizabeth I (reigned 1558-1603)

Elizabeth, queen at 25, had to restore faith in the monarchy and in a woman ruler, and to make the country prosperous, contented and safe. Her childhood was quite frightening at times; her own mother, Anne Boleyn, was executed when Elizabeth was only three. During her half-sister Mary's reign, Elizabeth was suspected of being involved in a rebellion against Mary's marriage to Philip, King of Spain. She pleaded her innocence in a letter to Mary.

I am by your council from you commanded to go to the Tower, a place more wanted for a false traitor than a true subject... I protest before God (Who shall be my truth, whatever malice shall devise), that I never practised, counselled, nor consented to anything that might be prejudicial to your person in any way, or dangerous to the state by any means... And as for the traitor Wyatt, he might peradventure write me a letter, but on my faith I never received any from him.

Elizabeth I, 1554

As queen, Elizabeth impressed many people, like Sir John Hayward, an author of historical works.
Now if any person had either the gift or the style to win the hearts of people, it was this queene.

Sir John Hayward, 1612

Elizabeth never married but liked the attention of male admirers, known as her 'favourites'. Elizabeth was vain and concerned with her appearance. Sir James Melville, an envoy from Scotland, described the queen and her need to know which queen was prettier, herself, the English Queen, or Mary Queen of Scots.

The Queen of England said she had clothes of every sort; which every day, as long as I was there, she changed. One day she had the English weed[1], another the French, and another the Italian, and so forth. She asked me which of them became her best. I said, the Italian dress; which pleased her well, for she delighted to show her golden coloured hair, wearing a caul[2] and bonnet as they do in Italy. She desired to know of me what colour of hair was reputed best; and whether my queen's hair or hers was best; and which of them two was fairest. I answered that the fairness of them both was not their worst faults. But she was earnest with me to declare which of them I thought fairest. I said she was the fairest queen in England and ours the fairest queen in Scotland.

Sir James Melville, 1564

1. **English weed:** clothes in the English fashion.
2. **caul:** attractive hair net.

Elizabeth was a great public-speaker. This is from her last speech to Parliament. Her robes were so heavy her tired body could hardly support them.

Mr Speaker... I do assure you that there is no prince that loveth his subjects better, or whose love can countervail[3] our love; there is no jewel, be it of never so rich a price, which I prefer before this jewel; I mean your love, for I do more esteem it than any treasure or riches... And though God hath raised me high, yet this I count the glory of my crown: That I have reigned with your loves. This makes me that I do not so much rejoice that God hath made me a queen, as to be a queen over so thankful a people.

Elizabeth I, 1601

3. **countervail:** balance out equally.

The Church and Religion

Religion was very important to people in Tudor times, but some criticized the Roman Catholic[4] Church for being wealthy and elitist. Henry VIII used these strong feelings about the Church to establish himself as its head in 1534. Henry had quarrelled with the Pope who would not allow him to end his first marriage to Catherine of Aragon so that he could marry a new queen, Anne Boleyn, and have a son to be his heir. As head of the Church, Henry could now marry who he wanted and take the wealth of the Church for himself as well.

So began the English Reformation[5] and struggles over beliefs. Protestants[6] wanted to read the Bible in English, and have church services in English – instead of the Latin of the Roman Catholic Church. Catholics resisted. In Edward's reign, the Protestants dominated. In Mary's, the Catholics ruled once more. Elizabeth had to stabilize things, and find a middle way that was not Catholic but not too Protestant either. To the Pope and to Catholics generally, she was a heretic[7], who ought not to be on the throne.

4. **Catholic**: see page 4.
5. **Reformation**: see page 4.
6. **Protestant**: see page 4.
7. **heretic**: a person who goes against the established beliefs of a religion.

Anti-church Feeling

Many people criticized the Church from the start of Tudor times. The Church was very wealthy, and people often thought it was more interested in power than holiness. The poet John Skelton expressed what many felt.

So many good lessons
So many good sermons
And so few devotions
Saw I never.

8. **clerk**: in this case, a cleric or member of the Church, such as a priest.

So many good works
So few well-learned clerks[8]
And so few that goodness marks
Saw I never.

John Skelton, c. 1500

Henry VIII Takes over the Church

Henry VIII became head of the Church in 1534 by an Act of Parliament.

Be it enacted by authority of this present Parliament that the King our Sovereign Lord, his heirs and successor kings of this realm, shall be taken, accepted and reputed the only Supreme Head in earth of the Church of England called Anglicana Ecclesia[1].

1. **Anglicana Ecclesia**: English Church.

> Act of Supremacy, 1534

Sir Thomas More, who had been Henry's chief minister, said that Henry's actions were wrong. He was imprisoned and executed in 1535 for treason.

I am accused of breaking the law made by Parliament. But I say that the law goes against God's law and the law of the Church. Therefore, I must not obey it. No-one can change God's law, and only the Pope can change the Church's law.

> Sir Thomas More, 1534

The Dissolution of the Monasteries

Money from the Church now went to the King instead of the Pope. Monasteries and other religious houses[2] were 'visited', or inspected, to see how religiously active – and wealthy – they were. This letter to Thomas Cromwell, Henry's chief minister, from John London shows how the Church's wealth could come into royal hands. London was one of Henry's 'visitors'.

2. **religious houses**: abbeys, nunneries, priories, convents, monasteries.

I have pulled down the Image of Our Lady at Caversham where unto was great pilgrimage. The image is played over with silver, and I have put it in a chest fast locked and nailed up, and by the next barge that cometh from Reading to London it shall be brought to your worship.

> John London, 1537

Violence was sometimes used, as on the following visit to Langdon Priory in Kent.

I stood a great space knocking at the abbot's door. I found a short poleaxe[3] and with it I dashed the abbot's door to pieces. And about the house I go with the poleaxe in my hand, for the abbot is a dangerous knave.

Jack London, 1538

3. **poleaxe**: long-handled axe.

The last steward of the richest abbey in England, Glastonbury, was called Jack Horner. The story is that, to please Henry VIII, the abbot sent his steward, Jack, to the king with a pie in which were hidden the title deeds of 12 Glastonbury manors. Jack opened the pie, took one title deed, and gave Henry the rest, as remembered in the rhyme.

Little Jack Horner
Sat in the corner
Eating a Christmas pie.
He put in his thumb
And pulled out a plum,
And said, "What a good boy am I!"

Nursery rhyme, 1539

The Bible in English

Parts of the Bible had been translated into English in the 14th century. Henry VIII decided that the more people knew the Bible in English the less they would support the Pope. So on 6 May 1541, he ordered that every parish[4] should own and use a particular English Bible known as 'The Great Bible'. However, church services were still in Latin.

The Lord's Prayer, now 450 years old, was put into English as part of the translation of the Bible.

Our father which art in heaven, hallowed be thy name. Thy kingdom come. Thy will be done in earth as it is in heaven. Give us this day our daily bread. And forgive us our trespasses[5], as we forgive them that trespass against us. And lead us not into temptation. But deliver us from evil. Amen

Lord's Prayer, 1540s

4. **parish**: area of land for which each church was responsible.
5. **trespass**: wrong doing.

Extreme Protestant to Extreme Catholic

The death of Henry VIII released a surge of pent-up Protestant[1] feeling. Under Edward VI, there was a strong Protestant push, known as iconaclism, to get rid of Catholic habits of religion including statues and pictures of saints and the Virgin Mary (icons). The Act of Superstition, in 1550, made even possessing pictures illegal.

Be it enacted ... that if any person ... has in their keeping ... any images of stone, timber, alabaster, or earth, engraved, carved or painted, which have previously been taken out of any church or chapel, or still stand in a church or chapel ... and if they do not before the last day of next June deface and destroy or cause to be defaced and destroyed these images, every one of them ... they will forfeit and lose to the King our sovereign Lord for the first offence twenty shillings[1].

Act of Superstition, 1550

During Edward VI's reign church services were officially conducted in English. The Archbishop of Canterbury, Thomas Cranmer wrote the first *Book of Common Prayer* in 1549. A second more Protestant book replaced it in 1552. It included advice on how to conduct the services.

To take away the superstition which any person hath or might have about the bread and wine, it shall suffice that the bread be such as is usual to be eaten at the table with other meals; but the best and purest bread that conveniently may be gotten.

Book of Common Prayer, 1552

Queen Mary made England officially Catholic[3] again – and did so ruthlessly. Three hundred Protestant believers were burned for refusing to say the Pope was head of the Church in England. The strongly Protestant John Foxe, in his *Book of Martyrs*, described Bishop Latimer comforting a frightened

1. **Protestant**: see page 4.
2. **shillings**: see page 5.

3. **Catholic**: see page 4.

Bishop Ridley as they were about to be burnt at the stake.

Be of good comfort Master Ridley. Play the man. We shall this day light such a candle, by God's Grace, in England, as I trust shall never be put out.

John Foxe, 1563

As Archbishop of Canterbury, Cranmer came under attack from Mary and at first signed six 'recantations', admitting his Protestant beliefs were wrong. Then he learned that even so, he was to be burned as a heretic[4] and in 1556 he was taken to Oxford. On the day of his death, he preached a dramatic sermon stating his true belief. At the point where this quote ends, Cranmer was dragged away to be burned.

I renounce and reject, because they are things written by my hand that are the opposite of the truth which I believed in my heart, things written in fear of death and to save my life if need be ... all such bills written or signed by my own hand since my degradation... And because my hand offended by writing what was opposite to what was in my heart, my hand will be punished first; if I come to the fire, it shall be burned first. And as for the Pope, I reject him as the enemy of Christ, and as anti-Christ, with his false teaching.

Archbishop Cranmer, 1556

4. **heretic**: see page 15.

5. **sacrament**: a special religious ceremony or rite conducted by a priest.

6. **Lord's Supper**: the Christian ritual of taking bread and wine. Also called mass or Holy Communion.

A Stable Middle Way under Elizabeth

After the upheavals of Mary's reign, Elizabeth needed to settle things down and stop the arguments, if she could. In her Act of Uniformity she made the *Book of Common Prayer* compulsory again.

If any kind of parson, vicar or other minister who is obliged to sing or say common prayer or administer the sacraments[5], refuses to use the common prayers, or wilfully or obstinately uses any other rite, ceremony, form or manner of celebrating the Lord's Supper[6], publicly or secretly, and is convicted of doing so according to the laws of the realm, he must suffer these penalties: for the first offence, forfeiture of one year's profit from his spiritual benefices or promotions, plus six months' imprisonment; for the second offence, one year's imprisonment and deprivation; for the third offence, deprivation and imprisonment for life.

Act of Uniformity, 1559

1. **Catholic**: see page 4.
2. **Protestant**: see page 4.

A very difficult question about Holy Communion needed settling. The Catholic[1] view that the bread and wine are miraculously changed into the body and blood of Jesus was rejected by Protestants[2]. Elizabeth found a way of allowing people to believe either view by adding the words 'in remembrance' to the words 'drink this'.

And the minister that delivereth the cup shall say: "The blood of our Lord Jesus Christ which was shed for thee, preserve thy body and soul unto everlasting life. And drink this in remembrance that Christ's blood was shed for thee, and be thankful."

Book of Common Prayer, 1559

In his *Description of England*, William Harrison described how churches had changed by the reign of Elizabeth.

As for our churches themselves, the bells, and times of morning and evening prayer remain as in previous times, except that all the images, caskets, little shrines, rood-lofts[3], and monuments of idolatry have been removed or taken down or defaced; the only exception are the stories depicted in stained glass, because of the shortage of new glass and its high cost... Finally, where there used to be a great partition between the choir and the main body of the church, it is now either very small or there is none.

William Harrison, 1577

3. **rood-loft**: wooden structure above the screen separating the nave and chancel parts of the church.

Puritanism

Extreme Protestants were called Puritans[3]. They kept Sunday free of work and play – and complained when others did not, as in this little sermon, published in 1574.

It is terrible to see the wicked boldness of those who want to be thought of as God's people, who make no effort at all to observe the Sabbath and keep Sunday sacred ... if they have business to do, even though there is no great need to do so, they cannot leave Sunday alone. They ride and journey on the Sunday. They have to drive and cart on the Sunday. They have to row and ferry on the Sunday. They have to buy and sell on the Sunday. They have to keep markets and fairs on the Sunday. They treat all days the same, working days and holy days are the same thing.

Sermon, 1574

3. **Puritan**: see page 7.

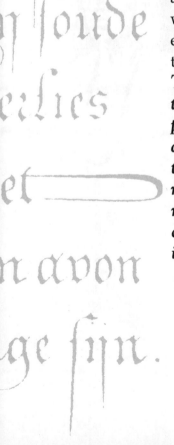

Magic

For people of Tudor times, religion was close to superstition, and it was easy to believe in wizards and fairies, the Devil, witches, and so on. Richard Scott, in *Discovery of Witchcraft*, explained how witches get air-borne from a drink made from the flesh of children who were not protected by religion.

Then the Devil teaches them how to make ointments from the innards and the flesh of children, which gives them the power to ride through the air, and do their ill-deeds. If there are any children who are nor baptised, or not guarded by the sign of the cross nearby, or by prayers, then the witches may take them away from their mother's side during the night, or out of cradles, and then kill them at a witches' ceremony. They steal children out of graves, and boil them in a cauldron until their flesh is liquefied and drinkable.

Richard Scott, 1584

Treason and Traitors

From Henry VII on, there were protests and rebellions against the Tudors, taxes, poverty, as well as agricultural and religious change.

Henry VII faced two 'pretenders', false claimants, to the throne in his first ten years. Then both he and Henry VIII faced protests when they tried to raise money for wars. When Henry VIII had taken over control of the Church, those who disagreed with the king in religious matters were guilty of treason.

Elizabeth had the Catholic[1] world for an enemy as Catholics wanted Mary Queen of Scots on the English throne. Spain, France and Scotland were ready to exploit her difficulties. In these rough waters, Elizabeth felt that the Tudor 'ship of state' needed stabilizers – a strong navy, watchful spies and a ruthless line with traitors.

1. **Catholic:** see page 4.

Threats to the Tudor Monarchy

In 1497, Perkin Warbeck pretended he was Richard, the son of Edward IV, in a challenge to the throne of Henry VII. A letter written by Raimondo de Socino, a Venetian living in London, described what happened. After his capture, Henry VII had Perkin imprisoned, and later executed.

On the 6th of this month Perkin landed in Cornwall at a port called Mount St Michael with three small ships and about three hundred persons of various nationalities, who had followed him for some time before. As he had so few with him, it is thought that the Cornishmen must have invited him. In fact eight thousand peasants were forthwith in arms with him, although ill-disciplined and without any gentlemen, who form the governing class of England. They proclaimed Perkin as King Richard, and they paid for the food which the commune provided them... They marched towards his Majesty, who did not hear of this movement until the 10th.

He goes on to describe how Perkin Warbeck was

22

eventually captured and brought to the king, who conducted a simple test.

The young man was brought into the royal presence, where many nobles of the realm were assembled, some of whom had been companions of Richard, Duke of York. He kneeled down and asked for mercy. The King bade him rise and then spoke as follows: We have heard that you call yourself Richard, Son of King Edward. In this place are some who were companions of that lord, look and see if you recognize them. The young man answered that he knew none of them, he was not Richard, he had never come to England except that once, and he had been induced by the English and Irish to commit this fraud and learn English.

Raimondo de Socino, 1497

Taxation and requests for money might produce discontent. In 1525, there was a rising in East Anglia when Henry VIII asked for money to pay for an invasion of France. Two of Henry's courtiers, the Dukes of Norfolk and Suffolk, wrote to warn him.

Please it Your Grace to be advertised that continually more and more knowledge doth come to us, that the confederacy with the evil disposed persons of this town extended to many places, not only in this shire and in Essex, but in Cambridgeshire, the town and university of Cambridge, and in divers other countries... And assured Your Grace may be that we will not depart hence unless that we see no manner of likelihood of new business as arise after our departure... And assuredly, all things well considered that we hear and see, we think we never saw the time so needful for the king's highness to call his council unto him, to debate and determine what is best to be done.

Dukes of Norfolk and Suffolk, 1525

Kett's rebellion in Norfolk in 1549 was against enclosures (see page 34), but the rebels asked for other changes too.

We pray your grace that where an act is passed for enclosing land that there should be no threat to those who have already enclosed land for growing saffron[1].

We pray your grace that no lord of no manor shall use the people's commons for his own common use.

We pray that reed ground and meadow ground be kept at the same price as they were in the first year of King Henry VII.

We pray that rivers may be free and common to all men for fishing and passage.

Rebels' Petition, 1549

1. **saffron**: valuable dye and flavouring obtained from the crocus.

Lady Jane Grey

In 1553, as Edward VI became very ill, his regent, the Duke of Northumberland feared that Edward's Catholic[2] half-sister Mary would become queen. He and Edward agreed to alter Henry VIII's will so that a cousin, Lady Jane Grey (who was Protestant[3]) would become queen.

When Edward died in July 1553, Jane became queen but, after only nine days, she was overthrown by Mary Tudor. Jane and Northumberland were both imprisoned in the Tower and later executed. Baptisa Spinola was a Genoese merchant who witnessed the political upheaval of those days.

Today I saw Lady Jane Grey walking in a grand procession to the Tower. She is now called queen, but is not popular, for the hearts of the people are with Mary, the Spanish Queen's daughter. This Jane is very short and thin, but prettily shaped and graceful. She has small features and a well-made nose, the mouth flexible and the lips red... The new queen was mounted on very high chopines[4] to make her look much taller, which were concealed by her robes, as she is very small and short. Many ladies followed, with noble men, but this lady is very heretical[5] and has never heard Mass, and some great people did not come into the procession for that reason.

Baptisa Spinola, 1553

2. **Catholic**: see page 4.
3. **Protestant**: see page 4.
4. **chopines**: a kind of shoe raised above the ground by very high soles.
5. **heretical**: see heretic, page 15.

Religious Up-risings against the Throne

When Elizabeth became queen and set up the Protestant Church again, English Catholics supported Elizabeth's cousin, Mary Queen of Scots, as rightful Queen of England. In 1567, Mary was forced off the Scottish throne by Protestants and she came to England.

In 1569, Catholics in the north of England staged an uprising in support of Mary. George Bowes, the Marshal of Berwick, described the siege at Barnard Castle in a letter to the government in London.

I found the people in the Castle in continual mutinies, seeking not only by great numbers to leap the walls and run to the rebels, but also by all means to betray the piece, and with open force to deliver it and all in it, to the rebels. So far, as in one day and night, two hundred and twenty-six men leapt over the walls and opened the gates and went to the enemy, of which number thirty-five broke their necks, legs or arms in the leaping.

George Bowes, 1569

6. **excommunicated:** thrown out of the Roman Catholic Church.

Elizabeth was excommunicated[6] by the Pope in 1570. After that she tightened religious security and instructed Justices of the Peace to look for 'papists', Catholics.

1572 Dec 28 York. Articles to be drawn up by the Council of the North to the justices of the peace. You are first to inquire and certify to us the names and addresses of suspected papists within your rule, the enemies of God and of good order, especially of such who do not come to church.

Elizabeth I, 1572

The Catholic Threat

Two government agents spent months tracking down Edmund Campion, a determined Catholic missionary. One of the agents, George Elliott, who wrote the following report, and his colleague, Jenkins, finally discovered where Campion was staying. Campion was arrested and executed for treason.

Jenkins, by God's great goodness, noticed a certain secret place, which he quickly discovered was hollow, and with an iron pin like the tine[1] of a harrow which he had in his hand he broke a hole into the space, where he saw at once the priests lying on a bed purposely set up there for them. And they had enough food and drink with them for three or four days' supply.

George Elliott, 1581

Elizabeth's Problems

For the Pope, Elizabeth I was a heretic[1] and a danger to the Catholic Church. He issued a statement supporting attempts to take her throne. In 1588 Elizabeth made a ringing speech to her troops assembled at Tilbury waiting to repel the Spanish Armada[3] sent to remove Elizabeth from the throne. She was warned the crowd might mean danger for her – 'treachery'.

My loving people, we have been persuaded by some that are careful for our safety to take heed how we commit ourselves to armed multitudes, for fear of treachery. But I assure you, I do not desire to live to distrust my faithful and loving people… Let tyrants fear. And therefore I am come among you, as you see, resolved, in the midst and heat of the battle, to live or die amongst you all, to lay down for my God, and for my Kingdom, and for my people, my honour and my blood, even in the dust.

I know I have the body of a weak and feeble woman, but I have the heart and stomach of a King, and a King of England too, and think foul scorn that Parma or Spain or any prince of Europe should dare to invade the borders of my realm. To which, rather than any dishonour should grow by me, I myself will take up arms, I myself will be your general.

Elizabeth I, 1588

1. **tine**: a spike. The tines on a harrow smooth the soil and cover the seeds after sowing.
2. **heretic**: see page 15.
3. **Armada**: see page 5.

The Secret Service

Elizabeth had to stay alert; three more armadas, in 1596, 1597 and 1599 were fortunately scattered by strong winds. But her secret service wasn't always efficient. A few years earlier, with three men on the run after a conspiracy, a trusted minister, Burghley, wrote to his superior, Walsingham, about seeing groups of watchmen doing nothing.

Sir, as I came from London homeward in my coach I saw at every town's end the number of ten or twelve standing with long staves[4], and until I came to Enfield I thought no other of them but that they had stayed for avoiding of the rain, or to drink at some alehouse… But at Enfield, finding a dozen in a plump, I bethought myself that they were appointed as watchmen, for the apprehending of such as are missing. And thereupon I called some of them apart and asked them wherefore they stood there. And one of them answered, "To take three young men." And demanding how they should know the persons, one answered with these words, "Marry my lord, by intelligence of their favour." "What mean you by that?" quoth I. "Marry," said they, "one of the parties hath a hooked nose." "And have you," I said, "no other mark?" "No," said they.

William Burghley, 1586

4. **stave**: long stick or staff that could be used as a weapon.

There was no mistaking the Elizabethan state's power, or its ruthlessness in punishing any threat to it. One of the first things German traveller Thomas Platter saw in London when he arrived in 1599, was this:

At the top of one tower almost in the centre of the bridge were tall stakes, on top of which were impaled more than thirty skulls of noblemen who had been beheaded for treason or other reasons.

Thomas Platter, 1599

Tudor People

Tudor society was often compared to a ladder of householders. On the top rung was the wealthiest person, the monarch, then in descending order came nobles, gentlemen, well-off citizens in towns, then the yeomen – the farmers with land of their own; on the bottom rung were wage-earning skilled workmen or labourers.

There were also people who weren't really on the ladder; they were part of someone else's household, as servants and 'bondmen' (effectively slaves). There were large numbers of these in rich households; the total number of these attendants and servants at Elizabeth's court was about 1500.

There was a huge gap in income between those at the top and bottom of the ladder. In 1535, nobles had an average income of over £1,000 a year, while in 1561, an average farm labourer would earn about 28s 6d[1] (£1.42p).

1. **28s 6d:** see page 5.

'Degree'

An inscription at Grafton Manor in Worcestershire says that harmony depended on different ranks, or 'degrees', being content with their place on the 'ladder'.

While every man is pleased in his degree
There is both peace and unity;
Solomon says there is no concord
Where everyone wants to be a lord.

Inscription, 1567

Crafts and trades had their social ranking, and their snobberies, as Thomas Nashe described in his book, *Piers Penniless.*

In London, the rich disdain the poor. The courtier the citizen. The citizen the countryman. The merchant the retailer. The retailer the craftsman, the better sort of craftsman the baser[2]. The shoemaker the cobbler. The cobbler the carman[3].

2. **baser:** less good.
3. **carman:** a man who drives a cart for a living.

Thomas Nashe, 1594

But Tudor people also believed that they could better themselves. Sir Walter Raleigh, in *Instructions to his Son and Posterity*, gives this advice to his son, comparing society with life on board ship.

Strive, if thou can'st, to make good thy station on the upper deck; those that live under hatches[4] are ordained to be drudges and slaves.

Sir Walter Raleigh, 1599

4. hatches: sliding doors leading to the space below deck on a boat.

The Court

The court put on lavish entertainments and displays, including hunting and bear-baiting. Music and poetry were important too. The courtier and diplomat Thomas Wyatt brought one amazingly popular import from Italy – a 14-line poem, the 'sonnet'. Once the court spread the fashion, Tudor poets wrote thousands. Wyatt was supposed to have written this to his 'deer' – 'dear' – Anne Boleyn, who is 'Caesar's' – the king's. In writing this, Wyatt risked Anne's life and his own; despite its splendour, life at court held many dangers.

Whoso list to hunt, I know there is an hind,
But as for me, alas, I may no more.
The vain travail hath wearied me so sore,
I am of those that farthest come behind.
Yet may I by no means my wearied mind
Draw from the Deer, but as she fleeth afore
Fainting I follow. I leave off therefore,
Since in a net I seek to hold the wind.
Who list to hunt (I put him out of doubt)
As well as I may spend his time in vain.
And, graven with diamonds, in letters plain
There is written her fair neck round about:
'Noli me tangere[5], for Caesar's I am,
And wild for to hold, though I seem tame.'

Sir Thomas Wyatt, c. 1530

5. Noli me tangere: No one touch me.

Elizabeth, like her father, Henry VIII, wrote songs and poems.

When I was fair and young and favour graced me,
Of many was I sought their mistress[1] for to be,
But I did scorn them all and answered them therefore,
Go, go, go, seek some other where,
Importune me no more.

Elizabeth I, undated

1. **mistress**: wife.

Elizabeth's court in particular was a place of elaborate formal court ceremony. Thomas Platter was fascinated by it.

One of the knights handed her some books, kneeling when he approached her, as did the Admiral and Lord Cobham, who were also present. I am told they even play cards with the queen in a kneeling posture.

Thomas Platter, 1599

Gentility

Though 'ranks' and 'degrees' were distinct, people were ambitious to better themselves. In 1551, Edward VI complained about the rise of the farmer and merchant to the rank of landed gentleman.

The farmer and the merchant become landed men, and call themselves gentlemen, though they be churls[2]; the artificer[3] will leave the town and ... will live in the country; yea and more than that, will be a justice of peace.

Edward VI, 1551

2. **churls**: peasants.
3. **artificer**: a skilled craftsman.

Merchants

Tudor wealth was also created by merchants travelling abroad. Richard Hakluyt gave these instructions to merchants of the Muscovy Company[4] visiting Persia[5].

In Persia you will find carpets made of roughly spun wool – they are the best in the world, and wonderfully coloured. You must go to the cities and towns where they make them, and devise a way of finding out details of the whole dyeing

4. **Muscovy Company**: see page 7.
5. **Persia**: modern Iran.

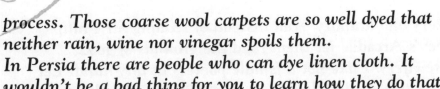

process. Those coarse wool carpets are so well dyed that neither rain, wine nor vinegar spoils them.
In Persia there are people who can dye linen cloth. It wouldn't be a bad thing for you to learn how they do that too. It was an established craft in England, and a few examples survive. But the skill has been lost, and can't be found anywhere in the country.

Richard Hakluyt, 1579

6. shillings: see page 5.
7. finical: fussy.

Rich merchants rose up the social scale. In *Piers Penniless*, Thomas Nashe described a rich merchant's wife who had 'arrived' socially.

Mistress Minx, a merchant's wife, who won't eat cherries till they cost twenty shillings[6] for a pound... She is so finical[7] in her talk it's as if she only spoke words she'd already sewed in her samplers... She spends half a day getting ready if she is invited out anywhere.

Thomas Nashe, 1592

Women

Women found it difficult to change the state they were born into. For Sir Thomas Smith, writer of *De Republica Anglorum* (*The English State*), women are on the same level as children when it comes to taking part in political life.

8. commonwealth: the public or whole body of people.

And in this consideration also we do reject women, as those whom nature hath made to keep home and nourish their family and children, and not to meddle with matters abroad, nor to bear office in city or commonwealth[8] no more than children and infants.

Sir Thomas Smith, 1583

Hugh Rhodes, in his *Boke of Nurture*, said that the arts and learning were fine for rich women, but not for 'a private gentleman's daughter'.

Instead of song and music let them [young ladies] learn

cookery and laundry. And instead of reading Sir Philip Sidney's Arcadia[1] let them read the grounds of good housewifery. I like not a female poetess at any hand. Let greater personages glory in their skill in music, the posture of their bodies, their knowledge in languages, the greatness and freedom of their spirits, and their arts in arranging of men's affections and their flattering faces: this is not the way to breed a private gentleman's daughter.

Hugh Rhodes, 1577

Labourers and the Poor

In the middle of the century the population was increasing. Prices and rents rose. Jobs were lost and unemployed people wandered the countryside and towns, begging. Being a 'vagrant' was made illegal. A court record from Middlesex describes one set of punishments.

29 March Elizabeth John Allen, Elizabeth Turner, Humphrey Foxe, Henry Bower and Agnes Wort, being over fourteen years old and having no lawful means of livelihood were vagrants and had been vagrants in other parts of the country. Sentenced to be flogged severely and burnt on the right ear.

Court Record, 1574

In 1570, the prosperous citizens of Norwich became worried about the growing problem of poverty in the city. They took a census of the poor, which told them that about 25% of the city's population needed 'poor relief'. Here are details of two families.

John Burr of the age of 54 years, glazier[2], very sick and work not, and Alice his wife ... 40 years, that spin, and have 7 children (aged 20, 12, 10, 8, 6, 4, and 2) who spin wool and have dwelt here ever – in his own house, no alms[3], indifferent[4]. John Findley, of the age of 82 years, cooper[5], not in work, and Joan his wife, sickly, that spin and knit, and have dwelt here ever – in the church house[6], very poor.

Norwich Census, 1570

1. **Arcadia**: a popular pastoral romance written by Sidney, a statesman and member of Queen Elizabeth's court.

2. **glazier**: someone whose job it is to put glass in windows.
3. **alms**: money or assistance given as charity.
4. **indifferent**: here probably means not so poor as some.
5. **cooper**: maker of barrels and tubs.
6. **church house**: one provided by the Church for poor people.

Farming and the Countryside

In Tudor England, most land was owned by large landowners and the king. They farmed some of it, and leased the rest to others, especially the class of yeoman tenant farmers. Beneath the landowners and the farmers came the class of farm labourers. They had no land of their own, only the right to use unenclosed common land for grazing animals.

The Tudor English countryside required many more different types of worker than now. Crafts and industries were located there, including cart-making, cloth-making and brick-making, charcoal-burning, iron-smelting and mining. And many more people than today produced their own food, or some of it, on small farms or pieces of rented land. Some of their produce would be sold locally, but food didn't keep and carts were slow; roads were badly maintained.

A Hard Life

Living in the Tudor countryside was hard work, as Shakespeare knew.

When icicles hang by the wall,
And Dick the shepherd blows his nail,
And Tom bears logs into the hall,
And milk comes frozen home in pail,
When blood is nipp'd, and ways be foul,
The nightly sings the staring owl,
Tu-who, Tu-whit, tu-who – a merry note,
While greasy Joan doth keel the pot.

Love Labour's Lost, William Shakespeare, 1594

Greasy Joan did a lot more than stir the pot to stop it boiling. A manual for farmers, Antony Fitzherbert's *Boke of Husbandry*, had an almost endless list of jobs for her of which these are just a few:

And when you are up and ready, then first sweep the house, set the table, and put everything in your house in good order. Milk your cows, suckle your calves, strain your milk, get our children up and dress them, and provide for your husband's breakfast, dinner, supper, and for your children and servants, and take your place with them. Send corn and malt to the mill so that you can bake and brew whenever there is need. Measure it for the mill and from the mill, and see that you have your measure again, less the toll[1], otherwise the miller acts dishonestly with you or else your corn is not as dry as it should be. You must make butter and cheese whenever you are able, feed your pigs both morning and evening, and give your poultry their food in the morning.

Antony Fitzherbert, 1525

1. **toll**: a fee, in this case paid to the miller.

The houses of country labourers were sometimes in a tumbledown state. The village court of Foxton, in Cambridgeshire, recorded the condition of some dwellings.
William Rayner has a barn and other buildings in a very ruinous state.
John Spencer's house and croft are seized for failure to do repairs.
William Ketell had not yet repaired his house.
William Rayner allowed his houses to fall down.

Court Record, 1500

Enclosures

The Tudor landscape was a changing one. The enclosures of late-medieval times continued to turn cultivated land into enclosed land for sheep-farming, which proved more profitable. Compared with growing crops, hardly any labour was needed. If labourers were not needed, neither were cottages for labourers. Some farmland returned to the wild; some villages were emptied. An anonymous popular song from about 1520 complained about houses being pulled down by landlords 'to pasture sheep'.

2. **sheepcote**: an enclosure for sheep.

*Great folk nowadays
Have a sheepcote[2] in the church.*

*Poor folk cry and weep
for their bread;
Towns are pulled down
to pasture sheep.
This is the style of things.*

*Merchants use subtlty,
the church lives viciously,
the commons are in poverty,
this land goes to waste.*

*Ploughmen dwell in the city,
Which will destroy the land shortly.*

Anon, 1520

3. **cardinal**: high-ranking member of the Roman Catholic Church.

In Sir Thomas More's book, *Utopia*, the character Raphael, a cardinal[3], and another, supposedly More himself, discussed enclosure as a cause for the rise in thieving. More said:
But this is not the only thing that makes thieving inevitable. There is another reason which I believe is peculiar to the English.
What is that? asked the Cardinal.
Your sheep, I answered. They are usually very tame and cheaply fed, but now, I hear, they have begun to be so greedy and uncontrolled that they devour human beings themselves and devastate and empty fields, houses and towns of people. In all those areas of the kingdom where the best and most expensive wool is produced, you find are noblemen, gentlemen and even some abbots – holy enough men in other ways – who are not satisfied with the annual revenues and profits which their predecessors derived from their estates. They are not content just to do no good to

their country by leading an idle and luxurious life; they need to do it positive harm. They don't leave any ground free to be ploughed; they enclose every bit of it for pasture; they pull down houses and destroy towns… Consequently, just so that one insatiable glutton can link field to field and surround thousands of acres with one endless fence, tenants are simply evicted. Some of them … are even stripped of their property, or else, worn out by the injustice of it all, they are driven to sell. By hook or by crook the poor wretches – men and women, husbands and wives, orphans and widows – are compelled to leave their own homes.

Sir Thomas More, 1516

There were several Acts against enclosures in Tudor times, including one during Henry VIII's Parliament in 1534. Thomas Cromwell, Henry's chief adviser at the time, sent him a note to let him know what had been decided.

It may also please your Majesty to know that yesterday a bill was passed in your Commons that from this time onwards no person in this kingdom may graze and nourish more than 2,000 sheep; also that an eighth of every farming man's land must be put under the plough every year.

Thomas Cromwell, 1534

Some enclosure continued through Elizabeth I's reign. One local observer saw the effects of the Bamfylde family's enclosure of part of Somerset in 1583.

Hardington village is completely enclosed and turned into pasture; and there is not a single house left standing apart from his own. He has pulled down the church, and it is hard to known where the parsonage stood, to which there belongs, it is well known, some glebe[1] land, but where that is will be discovered only with difficulty too.

Somerset writer, 1583

1. glebe: farm land attached to the parish church.

Industries, Crafts and Trade

Tudor England was a busy manufacturing country. Various crafts and industries still took place in the countryside, but a great deal also took place in towns, where more people began to live. Plymouth and Portsmouth were both fortified in Henry VIII's time and grew in importance. Other towns grew as a result of their cloth-making, or fishing fleets.

London was Europe's biggest city, with a population that grew from about 60,000 in 1520 to over 200,000 in 1600. The next largest, and the biggest manufacturing town, was Norwich, rising from 8,000 to 15,000 in the same period. Birmingham and Manchester were hardly more than villages, though they were growing.

London

The skill of London's craftworkers impressed Andreas Franciscus, an Italian visitor, writing to a friend in 1497.

There are also other great buildings, and specially a beautiful bridge over the Thames, of many marble arches, which has on it many shops built of stone. Throughout the town are to be seen many workshops of craftsmen in all sorts of mechanical arts. The working in silver, tin or white ivory is very expert here, and perhaps the finest I have seen. All the streets are so badly paved that they get wet at the slightest quantity of water, and this happens very frequently owing to large numbers of cattle carrying water, as well as on account of the rain of which there seems a great deal in this island.

Andreas Franciscus, 1497

2. **Protestant**: see page 4.

Immigrant Crafts

Many skilled workers arrived in England during Tudor times because of the persecution of Protestants[2] in Holland. In 1553, William Cholmeley wrote to Elizabeth describing his dyeing business – the only one in England, he claimed – which he and his Dutch workman had run for ten years. He wanted Elizabeth to dispel the belief that the water of the Thames and other rivers was not good for dyeing.

Among our products there is none that is in more need of being worked up by Englishmen than wool, because both cloth and caps are made from it, which everyone has to wear. For that reason I have tried to have the same articles made and then dyed within England by Englishmen, and as well as it ever was, or could be done in Flanders, or in France, or any other part of the world... And to achieve this, my first enterprise, I sent to Antwerp, and hired from there a man who is an expert in dyeing.

William Cholmeley, 1553

Since medieval times England had produced and exported wool and cloth. Now immigrant workers brought new skills or developed the old ones to add to the expansion of the growing towns and cities. Thomas Sotherton, Mayor of Norwich, describes in 1564 the value of workers from Flanders, who had revitalised working life in the city.

They do not only set on work their own people but do also set on work our own people within the city as well as a great number near 20 miles about the city, to the great relief of the poorer sort there. By their means our city is now well-inhabited, and decayed houses re-edified and repaired that were in ruin and more would be, and now good rents are paid for the same. They dig and delve a number of acres of ground and do sow flax, and do make it out in linen cloth which set many on work...

They obey all magistrates[1] and all good laws and ordinances; they live peaceably among themselves and towards all men, and we think our city happy to enjoy them.

Thomas Sotherton, 1564

1. **magistrates**: Justices of the Peace – local people who act as judges in local courts.

Anti-foreign Feeling

German miners in North-west England roused resentment. Elizabeth wrote a firm letter to Justices of the Peace in Cumbria after one nasty attack resulted in a death.

Certain Almayanes[2] privileged by our letters patent[3] under our great seal of England, with their great travail, skill and expense of moneys, have of late to their great commendation recovered out of the mountains and rocks within our counties of Westmoreland and Cumberland great quantities of minerals… They have lately been … assaulted, riotously and contrary to our peace and laws, by a great number of disorderly people in those counties, as a result of which there has been a murder of one of the Germans, which is likely to discourage the rest of them. We therefore and immediately order you to apprehend and safely detain all those who caused the said tumult or murder.

Elizabeth I, 1566

2. **Almayanes:** Germans.
3. **letters patent:** official document granting a patent, that is, an exclusive right or privilege.

In a letter home, written from Keswick, Cumbria in 1566, Daniel Hochstetter told Johan Lowver about his worries over persuading men to stay.

If no more measures are taken against the offenders than have been so far, I'm afraid that we shall not be able to keep our men for long … considering that they get no more in wages here, surrounded by danger, than they would at home, working in peace; the offenders parade daily in front of us, bragging and threatening our men with more trouble, especially that nasty individual, Fisher, who was the ringleader and chief instigator of the appalling murder of Leonard Stoultz, who fought to defend himself for a long time against twenty of them.

Daniel Hochstetter, 1566

The First 'Factories'

By the end of Elizabeth's reign there was evidence of quite large numbers of cloth workers being gathered in large single rooms – the first 'factories', perhaps. Thomas Deloney wrote a poem about Jack of Newbury in 1596.

Within one room being large and long,
There stood two hundred looms full strong:
Two hundred men, the truth is so,
Wrought in these looms all in a row.
And in another place hard by,
An hundred women cheerily
Were carding[1] hard with joyful cheer,
Who singing sat, with voices clear.

An din a chamber close beside
Two hundred maidens did abide.
These pretty maid did never lin[2],
But in that place all day did spin.

1. **carding**: part of the process of wool manufacture.
2. **lin**: cease.

Thomas Deloney, 1596

State Encouragement

The Tudors intervened to promote and regulate industry. Elizabeth used the sale of 'monopolies' – exclusive rights to manufacture a product - as a means of raising money.

Even a short list of these monopolies gives a glimpse of the variety of Tudor industry and trade.

30 Eliz – A patent[3] to Sir Walter Raleigh, to make licenses for keeping of taverns and retailing of wines throughout England.
33 Eliz – A grant to Reynold Hopton only, and no other, to make flasks, touch-boxes, powder-boxes, and bullet-boxes, for 15 years.
39 Eliz – A grant to Jon Spillman only, and no other, to buy linen rags, and make paper.

3. **patent**: see letters patent, page 39.

List of Monopolies, 1598-1601

Travel and Exploration

The Tudor era was a time of great exploration and new discoveries. Sir Francis Drake sailed right round the world; other travellers from England reached America and China, Russia, Persia[4] and India.

With exploration and travel came trade. New companies were founded to trade in all parts of the world, like the Muscovy Company[5] (1555), the Venice Company (1583), the Africa Company (1588), and the East India Company (1600). Ships returned to England 'richly laden with the commodities of China', Richard Hakluyt wrote. Ships sailed to Iceland and even Newfoundland for cod.

In Britain, travel by water was often easier than by land, though boats were sometimes unsafe. Crossing the English Channel was precarious, but there was frequent traffic, for trade, private travel, war and political reasons. One crossing, part of a journey to the Pope to try to get Henry VIII a divorce, took over four days.

4. **Persia**: see page 30.
5. **Muscovy Company**: see page 7.

Exploration

More and more Englishmen travelled abroad, to 'try their lot', wrote the poet Sir Richard Grenville. He was also the captain of *The Revenge*, the ship that held off 15 Spanish ships for 15 hours before Grenville was fatally wounded.

To pass the seas some think a toil,
Some think it strange abroad to roam,
Some think it grief to leave their soil,
Their parents, kinsfolk, and their home;
Think so who list[6], I like it not,
I must abroad to try my lot.

Sir Richard Grenville, c. 1580s

6. **list**: wish.

Christopher Columbus had asked Henry VII to support his voyage West in 1492. Henry refused, but in 1497 he

41

backed Giovanni Caboti (John Cabot). A Venetian, Lorenzo Pasqualio, wrote home to his brothers about Zaum (John) Cabot, who had crossed the Atlantic with 18 men, and landed on Newfoundland, which he later thought to be China.

Our Venetian, who went with a small ship from Bristol to find new islands, has come back, and says he has discovered, seven hundred leagues off, the mainland of the country of the Great Khan[1] and that he coasted along it for 300 leagues, and landed, but did not see any persons... His name is Zuam Cabot and he is called the Great Admiral ... and he goes dressed in silk. The English are ready to go with him, and so is an army of our rascals. The discoverer of these things has planted a large cross in the ground with a banner of England, and one of St Mark, as he is a Venetian; so that our flag has been hoisted very far away.

1. **Great Khan:** the leader of China.

Lorenzo Pasqualio, 1497

Between 1557 and 1560, Anthony Jenkinson led an expedition of English merchants and travellers to Moscow. With the Tsar's permission, they travelled down the Volga River and across the Caspian Sea to Persia[2]. One of the travellers, Giles Fletcher, described Russian winters.

2. **Persia:** see page 30.

The whole country in the winter lies under snow, which falls continually, and is sometimes a yard or two thick, but more towards the north. The rivers and other waters are all frozen up a yard or more thick, however broad or fast they are... Many people who are not even travelling far, but just out and about in the market or the street are fatally attacked by the cold, so you see people drop dead in the streets, and travellers who have come into the town sitting dead and stiff in their sledges... Many times, when the winter is extreme, packs of bears and wolves, driven by hunger, leave the forest and invade the villages, taking anything they can find.

Giles Fletcher, c. 1560

Trade

In 1563, by Act of Parliament, Elizabeth I said that everyone had to eat fish on Wednesdays, Fridays and Saturdays to promote the ship-building and fishing industry. By the end of the 16th century, a Newfoundland fishing fleet of 50 ships was based in Plymouth. Sir Walter Raleigh said this about them in 1595.

If these should be lost it would be the greatest blow ever given to England.

Sir Walter Raleigh, 1595

New scientific aims were part of some voyagers' outlooks. These 'notes in writing, besides more privie by mouth' were given by Richard Hakluyt to Charles Jackman and Arthur Pet, sailing for the Muscovy Company[3] to try to find the North-east Passage – north of Russia, to China.

3. **Muscovy Company**: see page 7

Also bring back the fruits of the countries you visit – if they will not keep, dry them and preserve them.
And bring back with you the kernels of pears and apples, and the stones of any fruits you find there.
Also bring home the seeds of any strange plants and flowers you find, because seeds from a distant part of the world will excite people's imaginations.

Richard Hakluyt, 1580

Round the World

In 1577, Sir Francis Drake set out to sail round the world. Some of his companions wrote about the three-year voyage. In these accounts, there was plenty of piracy and theft.

4. **Tarapaza:** a port on the Pacific coast of modern Chile.
5. **ducats:** Spanish coins.

We espied two ships under sail and gave chase to one... We boarded her from the ship's boat without resistance. We found her to be a good prize, yielding us a good store of wine. Then we came to a port called Tarapaza[4], where we found by the sea-side a Spaniard asleep, with 13 bars of silver beside him, which weighed 4000 Spanish ducats[5].

We took the silver and left the man.

Drake claimed what is now California and called it Albion.
Before we went from there, our General caused to be set up
a monument of our being there, as also of her Majesty's right
and title to that kingdom; namely a plate of brass, fast nailed
to a great and firm post; whereupon is engraved her Grace's
name, and the day and year of our arrival there ... together
with her Highness' picture and arms, in a piece of sixpence[1]
current English money.

1. **sixpence**: a coin worth half a shilling, see page 5.

Companion to Sir Francis Drake, c. 1580

Danger at Sea

Boats were not always kept in good repair, as Thomas Platter
discovered while crossing the English Channel.

We rebuked the captain in strong language for bringing us in
such a poor vessel, not above thirty paces long and ten broad,
with two decks all full of holes, so that we had to bale water
out with pumps all the time. To that he said he had no idea
things were so bad, and that after he returned to Calais with
the beer he would not use her again, but burn her.

Thomas Platter, 1599

The Dover-Calais crossing between England and France
might take three hours, or – with head-winds, storms, and
calms – three days. Platter was becalmed on his return
crossing.

Since the wind was more against us than in our favour we
made slow progress, and remained till midnight on the high
sea, when a calm befell us, so that we could move neither
way, except a little with the long oars which the captain
carried with him, enlisting all our services, but without the
wind our efforts were unfortunately not strong enough for us
to make great headway.

On the same return crossing, Platter came close to being
captured.

44

Our English captain warned us very earnestly not to make a noise, while he hid the light in our lantern so that we should not be seen, for he had sighted a Spanish ship from Dunkirk close by, which was patrolling the sea, but it did not spot us, for which we were very glad. Having escaped this peril and once we were sure of Calais harbour, the captain swore that if the Spaniards had given chase, he would sooner have flung away his ship, or risked making straight for land, even if it meant complete destruction, rather than surrender to the Spaniards. He knew what Spaniards did to English captives – and what the English did to Spaniards.

Thomas Platter, 1599

On the Roads

Travellers often found English roads difficult. In 1592, the German Duke of Wurtembourg travelled from London to Cambridge.

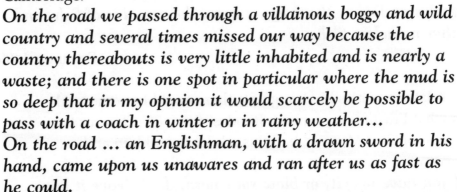

On the road we passed through a villainous boggy and wild country and several times missed our way because the country thereabouts is very little inhabited and is nearly a waste; and there is one spot in particular where the mud is so deep that in my opinion it would scarcely be possible to pass with a coach in winter or in rainy weather...
On the road ... an Englishman, with a drawn sword in his hand, came upon us unawares and ran after us as fast as he could.

Duke of Wurtembourg, 1592

At least English inns were welcoming, according to William Harrison in his *Description of England*.
In all our inns we have plenty of ale, beer and sundry kinds of wine, and such is the capacity of some of them that they are able to lodge two hundred or three hundred persons and their horses at ease.

William Harrison, 1587

Wealthy Households

By the end of Tudor times, many people's houses were probably becoming more comfortable, and perhaps warmer. But visitors like Erasmus noted how dirty they were. In Mary Tudor's time, one traveller remarked that English houses are made of 'sticks and mud' – wattle and daub, or West of England 'cob'. At the same time, many of the rich built very sumptuous houses of brick and even stone. These houses were like small palaces, kept running by armies of servants. It is about these wealthy households that most written records survive.

Houses and Comfort

Our standards of comfort are very different from those of Tudor times. Were floors of houses really like this, or was the scholar Erasmus exaggerating a bit in this private letter?

The floors are made of clay and are covered with layers of rushes, constantly replenished, so that the bottom layer remains for twenty years harbouring spittle, vomit, the urine of dogs and men, the dregs of beer, the remains of fish, and other nameless filth.

Erasmus, 1499

A later manners book suggests there might be some truth in what Erasmus says. Hugh Rhodes' *Boke of Nurture, or the Schoole of Good Manners,* had this advice to children and servants.

If you have to spit, or blow your nose, don't leave it lying there in sight of everyone, rub it out with your foot.

Hugh Rhodes, 1577

William Smith described how in his lifetime rural houses in Cheshire had become more comfortable – as for instance in the position of the fireplace.

In building and furniture of their houses (till of late years) they used the old manner of the Saxons. For they had their

1. **hob**: a flat shelf against the fireplace where pots can be warmed.

fire in the middest of the house against a hob[1] of clay, and their oxen also under the same roof. But within these 40 years it is altogether altered, so that they have builded chimneys, and furnished other parts of their houses accordingly.

William Smith, 1585

Servants

We get glimpses of life in a well-off house from a set of rules for servants. These rules were written for the master of a busy household.

2. **pence**: see page 5.

3. **trencher**: wooden plate.

Any servant who is absent without an excuse from morning or evening meals or prayers is fined two pence[2] each time.
Any servant late to dinner will be fined two pence.
Any man waiting at table without a trencher[3] in his hand, unless he has a good excuse, will be fined one penny.
For every swear-word, a servant is fined one penny.
Any man striking someone or encouraging someone to strike another person will be liable to be dismissed.
For a dirty shirt on Sunday or a missing button the fine will be sixpence.
After 8 am no bed must be left un-made and no fireplace or candle left un-cleaned, otherwise the fine will be a penny.
The hall must be cleaned in an hour.
Any man who leaves a door open which he had found shut will be fined one penny unless he has a good excuse.
The whole house must be swept and dusted every Friday.

Rules for an Elizabethan Household, date unknown

Marriage

In Shakespeare's play *As You Like It*, Rosalind – disguised as a young man – pretends to warn Orlando off marriage. He's in love with her. She's testing him – using the image of the 'difficult' wife popular with many Tudor moralists.

Rosalind [disguised]: *Now tell me, how long you would have her, after you have possessed her?*
Orlando: *For ever, and a day.*
Rosalind: *Say a day, without the ever. No, no, Orlando, men are April when they woo, December when they wed. Maids are May when they are maids, but the sky changes when they are wives. I will be more jealous of thee that a Barbary cock-pigeon over his hen, more clamorous than a parrot against rain, more new-fangled[1] than an ape, more giddy in my desires than a monkey. I will weep for nothing, like Diana in the fountain, and will do that when you are disposed to be merry. I will laugh like a hyena, and that when thou art inclined to sleep.*

As You Like It, William Shakespeare, c. 1600

1. new-fangled: excessively fond of new things.

But a Dutchman, Emanuale von Meteren, thought England was a 'paradise' for the relatively wealthy women he encountered.

Although the women are completely in the power of their husbands, they are not kept as strictly as they are in Spain and elsewhere, where they are shut up indoors. They go to market to buy what they want to eat. They are well-dressed, fond of taking it easy, and they usually leave the drudgery of housework to their servants. They sit outside at the door of their houses, dressed in fine clothes, so as to be seen by passers-by... All the rest of their time is spent walking and riding, or playing cards, talking with their friends (whom they call 'gossips') and neighbours, and celebrating with them when children are borne and at christenings, weddings, and funerals, all with the permission of their husbands... This is why England is called 'A Paradise for Married Women'.

Emanuale von Meteren, 1575

Bringing up Children

Learning good manners was a very important part of children's upbringing. These instructions, from Hugh Rhodes' *Boke of Nurture*, were for both children and servants.

Don't make a noise drinking soup... Don't dip your meat in the salt, take it with your knife. When you have eaten your soup, wipe your spoon clean, and place it on the table in front of your trencher[2], don't leave it in the dish... Don't tear your meat, that is far from being courteous. And if a visitor or stranger sits near you, every now and again offer him something tasty – be a gentleman. Don't scratch your head at the table, or spit... Don't pick your teeth with your knife or the end of your fingers, use a small stick or something clean. Don't fill your mouth too full so that you can't talk, or blow crumbs out of your mouth while you're eating.

Hugh Rhodes, 1577

2. **trencher**: see page 47.

In Rhodes' book, religion was the most important thing in children's upbringing – and reading: but religious books, not other kinds.

You ought to take them, often, to hear God's word being preached, and then ask them about what they have been listening to. Make sure they read the Bible and other religious books, and also that they don't read imaginary fables and silly fantasy stories, and stories and songs about love, which are bad for the young... And all of you who are their friends or related to them have to work hard to make them love you and fear you.

Hugh Rhodes, 1577

Food

Rich people enjoyed a lavish lifestyle with huge meals (Royal Household Accounts list 33,000 chickens, 20,000 sheep and lambs and 560 sides of bacon amongst the food consumed in one year). A yeoman farmer would have three good meals a day while a poor person had to manage with what they could get.

Thomas Platter said he had 'never seen more taverns and ale-houses in my whole life than in London'. In a book called *Journeys in Britain*, Andreas Franciscus commented on the size of the English appetite, and people's fondness for meat and beer.

They eat very often, at times more than is good for them, and they are particularly fond of young swans, rabbits, deer and sea-birds. They often eat mutton and beef, which is generally thought to be better there than anywhere in the world. This is because of the richness of their fields. They have plentiful supplies of all kinds of fish, and of oysters from the sea-shore. The majority drink beer.

Andreas Franciscus, 1497

Fish, especially that brought from a distance, needed salting or curing. The poorer kind of cod, which was cured and dried in summer, was called 'poor john'. In *The Tempest* by Shakespeare, Trinculo finds Caliban asleep on the beach.

He smells like a fish – a very ancient and fish-like smell – a kind of, not of the newest, poor john.

The Tempest, William Shakespeare, c. 1611

Tudor people ate various things that we do not. This recipe for 'sparrow broth' appeared in a *Book of Cookery*.

Take some good ale – a pottle[1], or some such amount at your own discretion, and put it on the fire to boil. Put the sparrows in and scum off the broth. Then put in onions, parsley, thyme, rosemary chopped fine, pepper and saffron, with a few cloves and some mace. Make sippets[2] as you do for fish, and place the sparrows on them, with the broth.

Book of Cookery, 1595

1. **pottle:** measurement of two quarts.
2. **sippets:** large squares of fried bread (croutons).

50

Schooling

When the monasteries were dissolved under Henry VIII, many schools attached to them disappeared. New schools were founded in their place, 18 of them between 1535 and 1547. The establishment of new schools continued and 136 grammar schools[3] were founded in Elizabeth I's reign.

3. **grammar schools**: see page 6.
4. **Herball**: a book about plants with medicinal properties.

Children of rich parents might be educated at home by a tutor, or sent away to be brought up in noble households. Here the main education was in good manners, the rest of the time being spent in learning to hunt, ride and fight.

There were many village schools, which took girls as well as boys. These schools concentrated on reading and writing.

Learning at Home

Many children did not go to school at all and were taught reading and writing at home. Girls received little education except in how to run a home and learn needlework. Grace Sharington of Lacock Abbey was educated by her aunt.

When she saw me doing nothing much, she would get me to do some writing with the pen and to add up and check sums and accounts ... at other times she let me read in Dr Turner's Herball[4] ... or she gave me some delicate stitching to do; she was an excellent workwoman in all kinds of needlework.

Grace Sharington, c. 1560

Unusually, Henry VIII believed in a good education for his children, boys and girls alike. Edward VI was admired for his ability with languages and knowledge of philosophy. His sister, Elizabeth, learnt Latin and Greek and was also a very clever student, as related by her tutor, Roger Ascham.

French and Latin she speaks like English; Latin, with fluency, propriety and judgement; she also spoke Greek with me, frequently, willingly, and moderately well.

Roger Ascham, 1570

51

Lady Jane Grey, Henry VIII's niece (see page 24), told Roger Ascham about her childhood where education was a refuge from strict parents. He recalled her words in his book, *The Schoolmaster*.

One of the greatest benefits that ever God gave me is, that he sent me so sharp and severe parents, and so gentle a schoolmaster. For when I am in presence either of father or mother, whether I speak, keep silence, sit, stand or go; eat, drink, be merry or sad; be sewing, playing, dancing, or doing anything else, I must do it, as it were in such weight, measure and number, even so perfectly as God made the world, or else I am so sharply taunted, so cruelly threatened, yea presently sometimes with pinches, nips and bobs[1], and other ways which I will not name, for the honour I bear them, so without measure misordered, that I think myself in hell, till time come that I must go to Mr Elmer, who teacheth me so gently, with such fair allurements to learning, that I think all the time nothing while I am with him. And when I am called from him I fall on weeping, because whatsoever I do but learning is full of grief, trouble, fear, and whole misliking unto me. And thus my book hath been so much my pleasure and more, that in respect of it, all other pleasures, in very deed, be but trifles and troubles to me.

Roger Ascham, 1570

1. bob: a slight blow.

Schools

By 1497 when an Italian, Andreas Franciscus, came to England, there were many schools. But he was not impressed by educational standards.

They show no trace of schooling (I am talking of the common people).

Andreas Franciscus, 1497

In his *Description of England*, William Harrison refers to the grammar schools and their system of fees. Most parents had to pay school fees for their children but the poorer ones could win scholarships and attend for free. Few grammars took girls, some were free to all.

There are a great many grammar schools throughout the realm, very generously endowed, to make better provision for poor scholars. Under the Queen's rule there are not many towns now that do not have at least one grammar school, with sufficient income to employ a master and an usher.

William Harrison, 1577 or 1587

Shakespeare went to the same kind of school.

...The whining schoolboy, with his satchel
And shining morning face, creeping like snail,
Unwillingly to school.

As You Like It, William Shakespeare, c. 1600

Most lessons were taught in Latin and too much English was seen to be a bad thing. Masters in schools wrote sentences for pupils to translate into Latin, such as this one:

If you cannot express the ideas in your mind in Latin, the only reason – there is no other – is that you use your mother-tongue more than Latin. That is what holds you back, and not just you, your school-mates as well.

School Record, Magdalen College, Oxford, c. 1500

The School Day

Some translation sentences tell us about school discipline.

I went to the town yesterday – a respectable fellow asked me to lunch. Afterwards I got away as quickly as I could, to be with you as your teacher, as I ought to be, but when I got back, I found there was no-one here to teach. So tell me, on whose instruction did you leave? Do you think that you can do whatever you like here without being punished?

School Record, Magdalen College, Oxford, c. 1500

The punishment would have been a beating. Erasmus of Rotterdam described the schools he knew.

The school is ... a torture chamber. Blows and shouts, sobs and howls fill the air.

Erasmus, 1529

Teachers were not well thought of, said Richard Mulcaster, Head of St Pauls School, London.

Our calling creeps low and hath pain for its companion.

Richard Mulcaster, 1582

A poem tells children how to be good pupils, and avoid punishments.

1. **Cato**: a writer from ancient Rome, died 149BC.

Remember your elders:
Cato[1] says that your elders
deserve respect and reverence
Young people must show
duty and obedience.

Remember your handkerchief:
Make sure you've got
a napkin ready
To clean your nose
when it gets dirty ...

And your equipment:
And before you go
have a good think
So you won't forget
pen, paper, or ink;
Those are the things
that are necessary,
They're the things
you need to carry.

Anon, 1557

Health and Medicine

By our standards, Tudor health-care was very primitive. There were very few doctors, and only the well-off could afford them. People died at a young age because living conditions were often bad and water was polluted. Many babies did not survive childhood. No-one understood how disease was spread

People relied on traditional cures, which were often magical: spring-water from the grave of a murdered man was supposed to cure the falling sickness. They went to the local 'wise woman'. They used plants and herbs, many of which probably worked quite effectively. And one or two thoughtful writers, like Andrew Boorde, stressed the importance of diet and laughter.

Epidemics and Plague

2. **plague**: a disease transmitted by rat-fleas from rats to people, causing high fever and buboes (swellings of the lymphatic glands).

Plague[2] was a regular visitor to England – which perhaps inspired this school-book sentence.

I was away from school a large part of last year because of the sickness that persisted in the town.

School Record, Magdalen College, Oxford, c. 1500

There were regular epidemics. In 1499-1500 a 'sleeping sickness' killed 20,000 people in London. The disease would strike suddenly, killing within a couple of hours. A French doctor in England saw what happened during the first of several outbreaks of 'sweating-sickness' during Tudor times.

We saw two priests standing together and speaking and both of them die suddenly. The wife of a tailor was also taken and died suddenly. Another young man walking by in the street fell down suddenly.

French doctor, c. 1510

Doctors

An Act of 1511, ordering that every surgeon or doctor had to be a university graduate, or else examined by experts, showed there were very few qualified doctors.

Every day in this kingdom, medicine and surgery are practised by a great number of ignorant people – ordinary workmen like smiths and weavers, and women with traditional remedies who boldly attempt the cure of severe medical problems, in part using sorcery and witchcraft, all of which results in considerable harm and hurt to our people, and even deaths.

Act, 1511

Advice about Health

In 1547, in his *A Breviary of Health,* the doctor Andrew Boorde reminded his readers that God was in charge of life, not science or medicine.

More than anything else I advise everyone who is sick, and anyone who has any infirmity, illness, or difficulty, to be at peace with himself, to arm himself with patience, and fix his heart and mind on Christ's death and passion[1] and to call to his remembrance what pains, what adversity, and what penury and poverty Christ did suffer for us.

Lords, ladies, and gentlemen, whether you are educated or not, and whatever estate or class of society you belong to, do not think, if it is the case that God has sent the sickness, that man can be helped by any kind of medicine, because He has given a length of time to every human being, which no-one can prolong by using any art or science.

He recommended good company, laughter and a good diet.

There is nothing that doth comfort the heart so much beside honest mirth and good company...

A good cook is half physician. For the chief physic (the counsel of a physician excepted) doth come from the kitchen.

Andrew Boorde, 1547

1. **passion:** the suffering of Christ on the Cross.

The healing property of herbs was well established and widely used at this time. Many people grew their own herbs for use in the household, for medicinal purposes or even to keep the house smelling clean, as noticed by Levine Lemnie, a Dutch doctor who visited England.

The neat cleanliness, the exquisite finesse, the pleasant and delightful furniture in every point for households wonderfully rejoiced me, their chambers and parlours strawed over with sweet herbs refreshed me, their nosegays[2] finely intermingled with sundry sorts of fragrants flowers in their bed-chambers and privy rooms with comfortable smell, cheered me up and entirely delighted my senses.

Levine Lemnie, 1576

2. **nosegay**: small bunch of sweet-smelling herbs and flowers.

Hospitals

Hospitals had traditionally been attached to monasteries and other religious houses. During Henry VIII's attack on the Church, many were taken over or closed down. Citizens of London presented a petition to Henry asking him to re-found three of them. The 'spitels' were more of a refuge for poor or sick people than hospitals as such.

... for the aid and comfort of the poor, sick, blind, aged and impotent persons, who are not able to help themselves, and have nowhere where they can be housed, looked after and made better till they are cured... For the assistance of these poor people, we inform your Grace that there are in the city of London three hospitals, or spitels, commonly called St Mary Spitel, Saint Bartholomew Spitel, and Saint Thomas Spitel, which were founded with great devotion by religious fathers of old and endowed with great possessions and rents...

If they were re-opened,

... a great number of poor, sick, needy and indigent[3] people shall be made better, looked after, comforted, found, healed, and cured of their infirmities, openly and freely by physicians, surgeons and apothecaries.

Petition, 1538

3. **indigent**: in extreme need; destitute.

Pastimes and Leisure

People enjoyed many leisure activities in Tudor times. Plays, music and dancing were popular as were sports such as bowling and archery. Some activities, such as tennis, hawking and hunting, were for the rich people. Other activities, such as cock-fighting and bear-baiting, that would today be regarded as very cruel, were enjoyed by everyone. In London, there were also theatres, taverns and gardens to enjoy.

1. **Puritan**: see page 7.

We can learn about entertainments not just from those who took part in them but also from those who disapproved of them, like the Puritans[2].

Plays

Plays were a great Tudor pastime. Travelling acting companies visited towns and cities, especially at the time of religious holidays, performing plays from the back of carts. Others visited playhouses, as described by Thomas Platter.

Daily at two in the afternoon London has two, sometimes three plays running in different places, competing with each other... The playhouses are so constructed that they play on a raised platform, so that everyone has a good view. There are different galleries and places however, where the seating is better ... and therefore more expensive. For whoever cares to stand below only pays one English penny[2], but if he wishes to sit he enters by another door, and pays another penny, while if he desires to sit in the most comfortable seats, which are cushioned where he not only sees everything well, but can also be seen, then he pays yet another English penny at another door.

2. **penny**: see page 5.

Thomas Platter, 1599

Puritans didn't like plays. John Northbrooke wrote a book called *A Treatise wherein Dicing, Dancing... and Vain Plays or Interludes are Reproved*. He said:

Many people can be at a play for two or three hours though they will not listen to even one hour of a sermon... If you want to find out how to be false and deceive your husbands or wives ... how to betray people, flatter, lie, break oaths, commit murder, administer poison, or ... rebel against princes; ... or how to attack and destroy cities and towns, how to be idle, how to blaspheme, how to sing filthy love-songs, how to be arrogant, how to sneer, and to deride and scoff at anyone in the world ... are not plays the way to learn how to do all these things?

John Northbrooke, 1577

The Fun of London

London appealed to many travellers. Just getting round and about the city, especially by boat, was a pleasant pastime.
The boatmen wait there in crowds... These wherries[3] are charmingly upholstered, with embroidered cushions laid across the seats, which are very comfortable to sit or lean on.

Thomas Platter also liked London's inns and taverns.
There are a great many inns, taverns and beer-gardens scattered about the city, where much amusement may be had with eating, drinking, fiddling and the rest – for instance our hostelry was visited by players almost daily.

Thomas Platter, 1599

3. **wherry**: a small, shallow boat.

Hunting and Tournaments

Hunting was 'the sport of kings' – few others could afford it. Women had a particular role, a German traveller, Philip Julius, Duke of Stettin Pomerania, noted in his journal.
The hunting parties are generally arranged in honour of the ladies. As soon as a stag or other animal is killed, the lady is expected to give it the first cuts with the hunting knife on the shoulder, the rest of the work being left to the huntsman.

Duke of Stettin Pomerania, 1602

Tournaments and pageants were held to celebrate great events, such as the birth of a royal baby. This pageant was held in 1512 on the eve of war against France. It went on to describe the tournament that followed.

First came in ladies all in white and red silk set upon coursers[1] trapped in the same suite[2] ... after whom followed a fountain curiously made of russet satin, with eight gargoyles spouting water, within the fountain sat a knight armed at all pieces. After this fountain followed a lady all in black silk dropped with fine silver on a courser trapped with the same. After followed a knight in a horse litter[3]. When the Fountain came to the tilt[4], the ladies rode round about and so did the Fountain and the knight within the litter.

Hall's Chronicle, 1512

1. **coursers**: horses.
2. **same suite**: same colours.
3. **horse litter**: a platform on which a person could sit.
4. **tilt**: site of a tournament.

Archery and Other Sports

For centuries kings encouraged men to practise at 'the butts'[5]. In 1529 a Lincolnshire village received this judgement from the Bailiff's court.

The targets called 'lez butts' are ruined and in decay. The villagers are ordered to repair them adequately before the 20th June next on pain of a fine of 6s 8d[6] if they fail to do so.

Court Record, 1529

5. **butts**: see page 9.
6. **6s 8d**: see page 5.

The Puritan[7] Philip Stubbes disliked archery[8] and other 'devilish pastimes', including football.

But some others spend the Sabbath Day [for the most part] in frequenting of bawdy stage plays and interludes; ... in May games, church ales, feasts ... piping, dancing, carding, bowling, tennis playing; in bear baiting, cock fighting, hawking, hunting and such like; in keeping of fairs and markets and the Sabbath; in keeping of courts and leets[9]; in football playing, and other devilish past-times.

Philip Stubbes, 1583

7. **Puritan**: see page 7.
8. **archery**: important skill for warfare, hunting and competitions.
9. **leets**: a local court held at a manor where information was given for records and taxes.

Tennis was a popular sport. Henry VII seems to have employed professional players for him to watch.

To a Spaniard; the tennis player £4
To the tennis player for ball   2 shillings
To the new player at tennis   £4

Royal Accounts for Henry VII, c. 1500

Music

Music, and learning to read and perform it, was an important part of Elizabethan life. The Duke of Stettin Pomerania, noted Elizabeth I's fondness for music.

The Queen keeps a number of young boys, who are taught to sing and to play on all sorts of musical instruments – they are also expected to continue their school studies at the same time. These boys have special instructors in the various arts, and especially in music. As part of their education in courtly matters they are required to put on a play once a week, and for this purpose the Queen has provided them with a theatre and a great deal of rich apparel... All the performances are by candle light and the effect is spectacular. For a whole hour before the play begins there is a concert of music for organs, lutes, pandoras[10], citterns[11], viols[12] and recorders.

Duke of Stettin Pomerania, 1602

10. **pandora**: early bass guitar.
11. **cittern**: small early guitar.
12. **viol**: stringed instrument.

Fashion

Tudor people enjoyed dressing with extravagant dash and colour. Philip Stubbes, in his *Anatomy of Abuses*, disapproved of men's high hats.

... sometimes standing up like the spear or shaft of a steeple, standing a quarter of a yard above the crown of their heads ... some of velvet, some of silk, some of wool and which is more, curious some of a certain kind of fine hair. These they called beaver hats ... fetched from beyond the sea.

Philip Stubbes, 1583

Timeline

1485 Henry Tudor defeats Richard III at the Battle of Bosworth, becomes Henry VII.

1486 Birth of Prince Arthur (heir to Henry VII).

1487 Lambert Simnel claims to be Edward, Earl of Warwick.

1492 Henry VII invades France.

1496 Henry VII gives financial support to John Cabot's voyage of exploration.

1496 Rebel Perkin Warbeck proclaimed Richard IV – he is later captured and executed.

1497 John Cabot sails from Bristol to Cappe Breton Islands.

1501 Prince Arthur marries Catherine of Aragon.

1502 Prince Arthur dies.

1503 12-year-old Prince Henry becomes engaged to Arthur's widow, Catherine of Aragon. The first English coin to carry a portrait of a monarch is issued.

1509 Death of Henry VII. Henry VIII marries Catherine of Aragon.

1511 War against France.

1516 Sir Thomas More's *Utopia* published. Birth of Princess Mary.

1520 Henry VIII meets King Francis I of France at the Field of the Cloth of Gold.

1522 War with Scotland and France.

1525 Peace with France.

1528 Plague (sweating sickness) in London. Henry seeking divorce.

1529 'Reformation' Parliament begins to pass laws reducing the power of the Pope in England.

1530 Thomas Wolsey, Henry's Chief Minister arrested and dies. Heretical books burnt in London, including Tyndale's English Bible.

1533 Henry VIII marries Anne Boleyn in secret. Cranmer made Archbishop of Canterbury – he pronounces Henry's marriage to Catherine void. Anne Boleyn crowned queen. Henry excommunicated by Pope. Birth of Princess Elizabeth.

1534 Henry recognised as 'Supreme Head' of English Church.

1535 Thomas More beheaded.

1536 Small monasteries dissolved. Cranmer declares Henry's marriage to Anne Boleyn null and void. Anne Boleyn beheaded. Henry marries Jane Seymour. Rebellion, 'Pilgrimage of Grace'.

1537 Birth of Prince Edward and death of Jane Seymour.

1538 Larger monasteries dissolved.

1539 'Great Bible' circulated to all parishes. Henry's 'Six Articles' are published – anti-Pope, but pro-Catholic.

1540 Henry marries Anne of Cleves – annulled after 6 months. Henry marries Catherine Howard.

1541 Henry becomes 'King of Ireland' and head of Irish Church.

1542 Catherine Howard beheaded.

1543 Henry marries Catherine Parr.

1545 Henry fighting at Calais.

1547 Henry VIII dies – succeeded by his son Edward VI.

1549 First *Book of Common Prayer*. Kett's Rebellion in Norfolk.

1552-3 Thirty-six grammar schools founded.

1553 Edward VI dies. Lady Jane Grey queen for 9 days in July, then Princess Mary, strongly Roman Catholic, proclaimed queen.

1554 Princess Elizabeth imprisoned. Mary Tudor and Pope on good terms. Wyatt's Rebellion against Mary's proposed marriage to Philip of Spain. Queen Mary marries Philip of Spain. Bishops Latimer and Ridley burnt at the stake.

1556 Archbishop Cranmer burnt at the stake.

1558 Mary dies.

1559 Coronation of Elizabeth who becomes head of the English Church. Second *Book of Common Prayer*.

1562 Elizabeth I ill with smallpox.

1563 Plague – 20,000 die in London. Foxe's *Book of Martyrs* published.

1566 Future James VI and I born to Mary Queen of Scots and Darnley.

1567 Darnley killed – Mary imprisoned.

1568 Mary Queen of Scots flees to England. Spanish capture English ships off Mexico and confiscate treasure. Spanish ships in Plymouth have treasure seized.

1569 Mary put under house arrest.

1570 Elizabeth I excommunicated by Pope.

1571 Act declaring all instructions from the Pope treasonable.

1572 House of Commons wants Elizabeth to execute Mary Queen of Scots – Elizabeth refuses.

1576 The Theatre opens, London's first playhouse.

1577 Drake leaves Plymouth to sail round the world.

1581 Heavy fines imposed for hearing Mass and non-attendance at church. Campion executed at Tyburn.

1583 St John's colony established on Newfoundland.

1585 Roanoke Island colony in North America.

1586 Babington Plot against Elizabeth. Queen Mary on trial for treasonable letters. Mary sentenced to death.

1587 Mary Queen of Scots executed.

1588 Spanish Armada sets sail, attacked, scattered.

1592 Plague in London – 17,000 deaths.

1593-95 First productions of several Shakespeare plays.

1598 Rebellion breaks out in Ireland.

1599 Earl of Essex signs unauthorised truce with rebels in Ireland.

1601 Earl of Essex leads rebellion – defeated and executed.

1603 Death of Elizabeth – James VI of Scotland becomes James I of England.

Index